Say The Quiet Part Out Loud

Liberate Your Inner Changemaker

Bina M. Patel

Say The Quiet Part Out Loud: Liberate Your Inner Changemaker
Copyright © 2023 by Bina M. Patel
www.saathiimpact.com

All rights reserved. No part of this book may be reproduced in any form or by any means without permission in writing from the publisher.
This book is not intended as a substitute for advice from a trained professional.

Printed in the United States of America.

Content Editor: Martha Cecilia Ovadia, La Libertad Consulting
Copy Editors: Chisom Ezeh, The Publishing Pad and Martha Cecilia Ovadia
Graphic Designer: Bina M Patel, Martha Cecilia Ovadia, Chisom Ezeh
Typesetting: Chisom Ezeh
Cover designer: Dea Biličič
Author Photographer: Pete Nagy

Published by The Publishing Pad
New Brunswick, Canada, E2P 1J3
www.thepublishingpad.com

ISBN: 9798987131589 (Paperback)
ISBN: 9798987131596 (eBook)

Say The Quiet Part Out Loud

Liberate Your Inner Changemaker

My labor is my joyful protest.

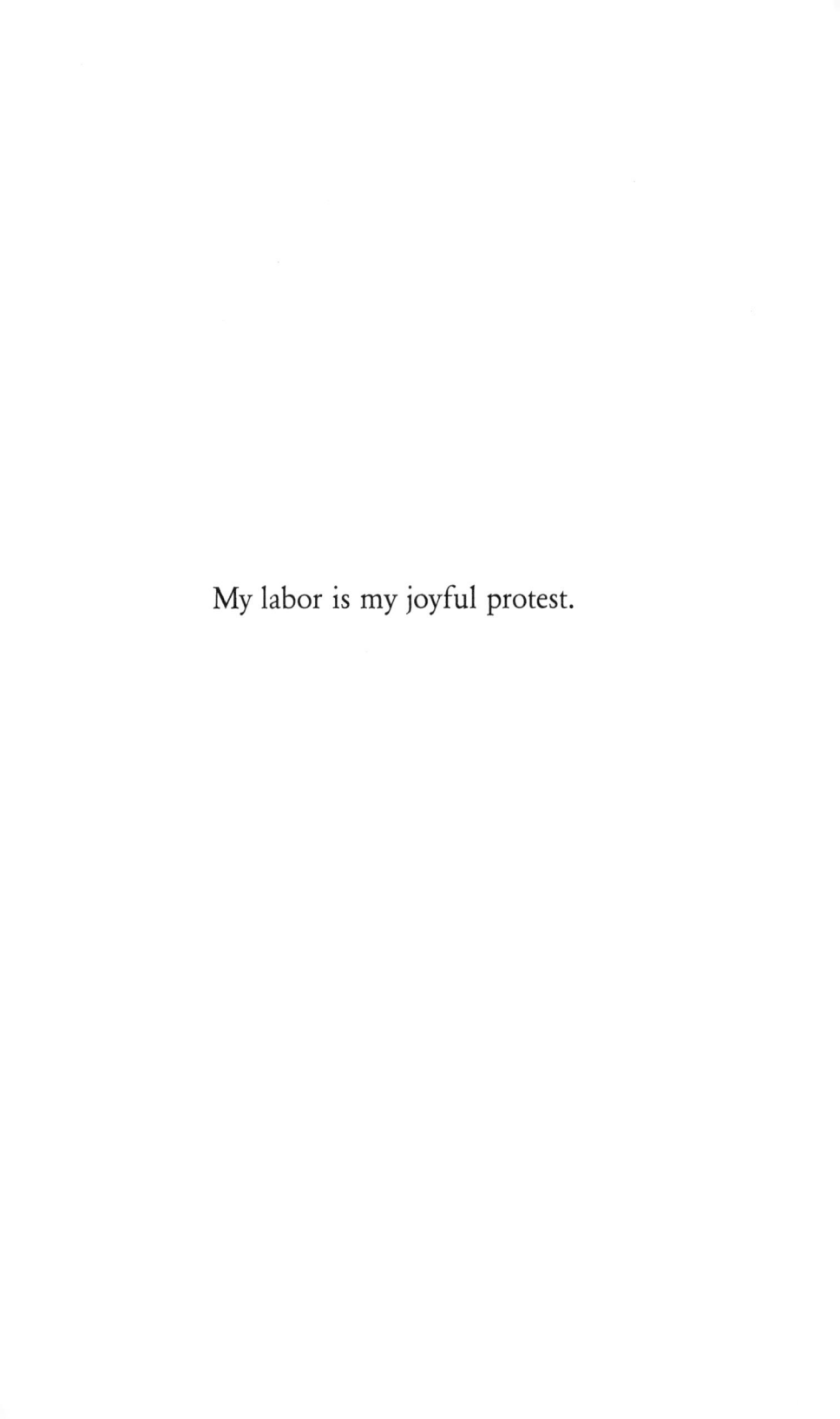

Offerings

Acknowledgment 2
Author's Welcome 3
    How to Use This Book 5
The Collective 8
Say the Quiet Part 10
    "_____" 13
        Encumbered 18
        Fear 21
        Love, Rage, and All of the Things 26
        Radicalize Your Rage 30
        On Why It Hurts 35
        Strategic Compliance 41
Rooted in Purpose 55
        Purpose 56
        Letting Go 66
        Unencumbered 68
        Agency 78
        Presence 86
        Healing 90
        John Chief Moon 94
        Jalebi and Hard Truths 105
Onwards, Together 111
        Find Your People 112
        Rest 113
        The Mountain 115
        Radical Possibility 123
        We Walk Together 137
Keep Going 141
Gratitude 143
Converse with Care 145
Reviews 147

If you don't want to change the world, don't turn the page.

Acknowledgment

This book was written across the gorgeous terrain of Southern California, primarily in Hakutl (Encinitas), on the lands of the Kumeyaay people, also known as the Tipai-Iipai Diegueño tribes. The Kumeyaay Nation has inhabited this area that spans Northern Baja into Southern California, separated by the US-Mexico border, for over 12,000 years. Kumeyaay means "those who face the water from a cliff." The current population of Kumeyaay is estimated at 20,000 people.

I also spent time on the desert lands of Cahuilla Territory, specifically the Agua Caliente Band of the Cahuilla Indians, who steward over 31,500 acres of ancestral lands in the region. Their history dates back over 5,000 years ago in this area, encompassing the deserts of the Coachella Valley and the valleys and mountains of the San Bernardino and San Gorgonio ranges.

I am grateful for the inspiration, quietness, lessons, and nourishment that comes from being on these lands. Hand to heart for the many Indigenous Peoples who have taught me lessons of strength, community, resilience, and solidarity and showed me love along the way.

To learn about the lands you live on, visit Native Land Digital[1]. They are Indigenous-led and have operated since 2015 with the mission to "...map Indigenous lands in a way that changes, challenges, and improves the way people see history and the present day. We hope to strengthen the spiritual bonds that people have with the land, its people, and its meaning."

With acknowledgment comes responsibility. To **say the quiet part out loud** is to center a way of being that honors our humanity and to actively make daily choices that work to eradicate the multifaceted, systemic, and painful ways many of us are made to live in the margins.

---

1   https://native-land.ca/

Author's Welcome

Hello friends!

We've been at this for a long while – at this work of co-creating and dreaming into a better world.

And we have a long way to go.

I think some of what we need is the space, energy, and encouragement to reconnect with ourselves and one another so that we can keep going together.

This book is about the power of **saying the quiet part out loud**, and what happens when we do this together.

I am regularly surrounded by amazing people who are deeply invested in the work of a more liberated today and tomorrow. In the last few years, I started to hear a phrase come up over and over again among friends, colleagues, and myself. We kept saying: *"I can't do this anymore."* I heard this from so many powerful changemakers, activists, and champions about how they felt defeated. It broke my heart.

I wrote this book for all of us, myself included. For everyone who is feeling defeated and about to give up.

In my line of work as an anti-oppression coach and facilitator, one of the ways I contribute to changemaking is to name the dynamics of the world in plain language and to offer pathways for folks to reconnect with their fierceness, vision, purpose, and voice.

Too often, many of us who are so deeply committed to a vision of a shared future rooted in love and justness are told we are too radical and unrealistic. We are told we just don't understand what reality is and what is possible.

I reject this. Those before me have rejected it as well.

I'd like for you to think of this book as a "coach in your pocket" – here to offer how I have learned to show up differently so we can show up to change the world, together. I want to share some of the lessons and methods that I've seen help bring folks back to their rootedness and strength.

Profound moments of being seen – actually being seen after so much of being *unseen* in our daily work and efforts spark action, purpose, and courage.

I see you.

How to Use This Book

Like a tapestry, there are many threads to pull from in this book that offer a way to recenter and free yourself from the distractions that take you away from your deeper work and present different framing and energy to your day-to-day work.

My hope is that you can pull on one or every thread, depending on what you need, when you reach for this book.

The first part of this book about naming the problems that require us to be changemakers was challenging to write and brought up so many emotions. But I felt these words needed to be said and seen.

The second and third parts of this book? Well, that is where the joy is in creating, building, and turning our labor and hearts to the deeper and more meaningful work of moving towards a more beautiful future.

So, as you read and use this book, it might be useful to think of it in three parts:

> **Part One: Say the Quiet Part**
>
> **Part Two: Rooted in Purpose**
>
> **Part Three: Onwards, Together**

On Reflections and Pauses

Throughout this book, you will find guided reflections that will prompt you to reflect deeply via journaling, drawing, or however else you tactically like to reflect.

Do what feels right.

There are also pauses for you to take a breath or two through guided breathwork. The hope is that you find space to pause and rest, reconnecting with your fierceness and purpose so that you can show up in ways that feel meaningful for you. Reflections, breathwork, and pauses can create space for growth. However, they can also ask us to delve deeper into and revisit experiences of trauma and harm. This is not a linear or easy journey. Please, take good care of yourself. Remember, there is no request in this book or work to retraumatize yourself. Find support and rest as needed in your journey. If it gets hard, take a break and return to it later.

You will find references throughout this book using terms related to anti-oppression, but this book is not focused on the conceptual or theoretical underpinnings of that work.

This is a book about how we show up to change these conditions. It is about how we recenter and unencumber ourselves from the notions of what it means to be a disruptor of the status quo. It is also about how to move more deeply and sustainably to undo what seems inescapable when the status quo tells the story.

TLDR: We've got this and we can do this.

Let's say the quiet things out loud, **together**.

In solidarity,

Bina

This book is for those who say the quiet part out loud.

The Collective

This book is an intimate and communal exploration for:

status quo disruptors	co-conspirators
abolitionists	edge-walkers
freedom fighters	healers
civil rights leaders	strategists
farm workers	activists
water protectors	radicals
Elders	truth-tellers
knowledge keepers	rebels
human rights activists	changemakers
feminists	agitators
queer liberators	allies
accomplices	community builders
youth truth-tellers	advocates

When I talk about the collective, I am talking about all those above and those who have yet to emerge, those who are willing to walk towards a vision that hasn't yet been painted but that we know we can create.

THERE
IS
ANOTHER
WAY

Say the Quiet Part

Naming it frees us and gives us power.

Call it what it is, and it will be seen.

Naming is the act of acknowledging what we see and experience by its purest and simplest name – this includes both the problems we are trying to address and the vision for what is radically possible.

Let's say the quiet part out loud by
naming the problem that brought us here.

THE FUCKERY.

"   "
_____

The Fuckery is all of the persistent, systemic, intersecting, and evolving ways that status and superiority play out: race, gender, ways of thinking and moving, ableism, fatphobia, class, religion, and sexual identity.[1] It disconnects us from ourselves and each other and lies to us about what the future can be.

I call it The Fuckery because it is that horrific. It is so violent and pervasive that there is almost no other language for the inheritance of western, patriarchal, ableist, cis, hetero, colonizer, imperialist, white supremacy. It seeps into everything and turns them toxic, poisonous, and deadly.

It is awful, hypocritical, insipid, frustrating, traumatic, maddening — it is The Fuckery of it all. It is "fragile" in the way that the sharpest edge of a broken fragment of glass is fragile. It has left us with a shattered image of our collective humanity.

And then, to add to the violence, this is all somehow made to feel normal. We are told that there is "nothing to see here!" and to move along.

We have the opportunity to undo The Fuckery and redefine how we are, together. This way of being is not ordained or destined.

_____

1   Did this make you gasp or feel some nervousness? Ask yourself why it caused such discomfort, and then let's keep going.

This is The Fuckery we are here to dismantle:

white supremacy	white fragility[3]
superiority	"It's been worse"
whiteness[1]	not all white people
dehumanization	all lives matter
disconnection	model minority
colonization	missionaries
patriarchy	white saviors
scarcity mindset	indoctrination
body policing	imposter syndrome
either/or thinking	unlivable wages
complacency	colorism
microaggressions[2]	objectivity
comfort vs. progress	loss of human rights
us vs. them	status quo
expat vs. immigrant	reverse racism
profit over people	narcissism
laziness	assimilation
exclusion	compartmentalizing
alt-right	professionalism
gaslighting	gender roles

---

1   The cultural behaviors, norms, and practices that uphold a system of white supremacy and The Fuckery, in which white people and people who are racialized are implicated, albeit in very different ways and for different reasons.
2   The impact is not micro.
3   It's not fragile. It's ferocious and harmful. It's white violence.

embedded biases	power asymmetry
christo-facism	credentialing
hypocrisy	dismissing
command and control	diminishing
weapons and militarization	erasure
demonizing	theft
your hair isn't right	hurt
white tears	harm
antisemitism	perfectionism
tone-policing	tokenism
conformity	domination

There is another way, and it is up to us to make it.

Reflect

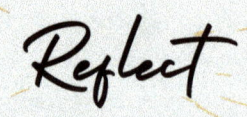

Naming the experiences we have lived through matters. It is healing to name and bring to light the many ways in which we have experienced The Fuckery (or have participated in it). In this space, say it out loud.

Let this piece of paper hold your stories so you can release the weight of carrying them.

Encumbered

Burden. Cramp. Hinder. Impede. Inhibit. Stifle. Suffocate. Suppress. Block. Bind. Constrain. Colonize. Conform. Pressure. Oppress. Encumber.

Being burdened by the weight of The Fuckery is a full-body experience, like those moments when you have the weight of the world on you and it feels like an anchor or when you feel yourself shrink to be smaller and take up less space. Or when you feel rage simmering inside, but you silence yourself. You know those moments when you feel your throat tighten as you swallow your words, change your hair, or practice limiting your accent when you speak? When you back down from sharing big ideas?

We all know this feeling because it is pervasive and shows up in different ways for most of us.[1]

---

1 Importantly, we all work to adapt to the environments we are in. All of us navigate our own identities in shared spaces. However, it is important to understand that the many types of code switching required by people of colors is explicitly due to systemic racism and systemic oppression within white-dominant, cis, hetero-normative, able-bodied normalized spaces.

Pause

Take a moment.

Taking a pause is important, given the hustle and grind we live in. The pause helps us be present, helps us relax, and gives us a chance to take a breath. Pausing helps us determine how we respond.

We often want to jump immediately into fixing and responding to the problems of The Fuckery. We are primed (indoctrinated!) into this pattern of urgency to fix and respond.

The pause is a practice of reclamation and release.

Reading through that list of The Fuckery and seeing your own stories is a lot, and it triggers deep responses. But it is important that we move through those emotional responses and not let them get stuck in us.

Here is a practice to manage some of that stress and your emotional response.

You may notice that after reading about The Fuckery, your breath becomes shallow, your jaw is clenched, and your heart is racing.

Start by standing up and taking a few deep breaths. Feel your breath in your lungs and belly.

Slowly begin to twist your trunk, letting your arms helicopter around you. Let your limbs feel heavy and swing freely. Stay with those deep breaths as you feel your arms wrap around you like a little hug.

Take a few minutes to just let your body turn back and forth (within your capacity), your arms wrapping around you as you twist. Keep your feet rooted. Don't force your body beyond what feels good at this moment.

After a few minutes of this, let your body come to a rest. Shake your arms and hands, roll your shoulders, and shake your ankles and feet.

Deep breath. Maybe one more.

Now stand up tall, feet planted to the ground and roll your shoulders back to open up your heart space. Embrace that feeling of taking up more space, your blood flowing through you, your breath bringing you expansion.

A last part of this practice is to let your hands dangle at your side, palms wide open, as you visualize the garbage of The Fuckery that is not yours to carry dropping away. Let it go; drop it to the ground.

Take a step forward. You are here now.

Modification: In any way you can comfortably center your body and mind, focus on your breath and how it feels within your body, letting the tension flow out as you center on breathing, pausing, and embodiment.

Fear

Changing the world is always scary. This work is always on the edge and just past the edge – past comfort zones and what is known. It is almost always fear-inducing. Systems of oppression are not known for inviting change.

The response to fear is not courage. It is purpose.[1]

Fear comes from knowing that there will be consequences when we step out of compliance. It also comes from being afraid to make a mistake, of saying the wrong thing. Fear is wrapped up in the context of compliance; with systems of oppression. We are often paralyzed and silent while regularly trying to be braver but not actually showing up for those who need us to show up.

Fear in changing the world is often contextualized by racial and power dynamics. Who has set the rules and boundaries? Who has the authority to retaliate?

Consider: Who is centered in these internal deliberations clouded in fear? Who are you keeping comfortable? Whose rules are you following?[2]

---

1 More on purpose in an upcoming chapter called Rooted in Purpose. Skip ahead or hang tight.
2 I often hear about fear of making a mistake or upsetting people. That fear of imperfection is rooted in white supremacy and reinforces self-protection instead relationship, learning, and practicing. There is a difference in the fear of retaliation for disrupting versus the discomfort of being corrected when making a mistake. It's whiteness that teaches retaliation. I've been corrected in my language or approach before - which has made me a better ally. And it was also noted with the acknowledgment that at least I was trying.

Very often, we find that we are afraid of decentering the status quo.

There are other kinds of fear as well: continuing hikes when the edge of the trail seems a bit narrow and falling into a 1,000-foot crevice? Facing tormentors in courts of law knowing there are no safe zones or allies in the space? 'Fessing up to mistakes and knowing the risks? So many things require bravery. But this work, in particular, requires us to look at fear with different eyes and meet the fear with purpose.

So, when you feel fear (and there is real fear to be felt in this work for those of us who are not at the top of the hierarchy), reconnect with your purpose. Who are you here for, and who do you walk with?

You can be afraid and purposeful.

The response to fear is not courage.

It's purpose.

Reflect

What are you practicing: fear or purpose?

Love, Rage, and All of the Things

I'd like to offer some space for rage. Dominant culture demonizes rage and often looks down upon those experiencing it as immature, naive, out of control, and violent. We are often told, "...just calm down!"

But rage is more dynamic than this. It is more useful. It has more purpose. We must be able to reach toward the edges of our rage and let it serve as light and fuel. Rage is an opening to action rooted in justice and activated by a desire to serve the collective good. For rage to be rooted in purpose, it must be of service of liberation — both communal and self. You can stay with it, feel it, and not erase this rage.

The grief, exasperation, and frustration of bearing witness again and again. Together, these show up as rage.

Rage, love, and grief — they live together. They exist together. Though truly not the same, we are not strangers to the range of emotions that are present as teachers in the work of changing the world.

Rage is a signal that we are in a relationship with one another and we are seeing each other. And that, dear friends, is love.

Rage makes us aware of injustice, reminding us of our shared humanity — even if we are not the ones directly experiencing the harm. Rage as a signal of love tells us that we are present for a reality that is challenging to be with, a reality that often breaks our hearts.

Rage, once felt and accepted without the weight of how the world perceives it, must be channeled into collective service, protest, and rebuilding.

To be of service, we must resist the urge to shrink, to let unchecked rage eat us up and turn us to ash.

*If rage is not a natural response to everything we are bearing witness to, are we even **being** this work?*

I wonder why more people aren't enraged. And then I wonder, do they know how to love?

To do this work, you have to be *in it* — in your heart, soul, cells, muscle memory, and synapses. You have to let what you bear witness to change you.

I had to unencumber and recenter my rage. This takes work and it can be exhausting. It has taken practice[1] to be in my body and to stay with the rage, not crumbling under its weight.

It took eventually coming to a place in which I let what I saw and felt change me.

I let the rage become fuel for holding more space for those who bear the direct pain and suffering of oppression and taking up space in a world guided by white supremacy that is always telling me to be smaller. We cannot lose our purpose in the face of the paralyzing rage we feel.

Rage makes us more honest, aware, and present to the urgency in this work. It creates action where helplessness used to live, and it connects love to purpose and confidence where there was once only

---

1 Through breathwork, finding places to more explicitly be an ally and accomplice, to advocate more publicly, to send donations to folks. It looks different for each of us.

silence. Rage is a practice of love. Rage is also a form of labor - good labor. It has purpose.

I invite you to let the rage of those moments you feel rage at the injustices you bear witness to change you again and again.

Let rage radicalize you and show the world how deeply you can love.

I WONDER
WHY MORE
PEOPLE AREN'T
ENRAGED?

**AND THEN I
WONDER: DO
THEY KNOW
HOW TO LOVE?**

Radicalize Your Rage

"How is this moment changing you?"

This was a check-in question on a webinar I spoke at during the summer of 2020. It left me struggling with tears welling up in response to the overwhelming nature of recent events that was weighing heavily on me.

When I dug a bit deeper, I was able to identify that what I called exhaustion was actually rage. I needed to confront the depths of my own rage at the unrelenting racism we are witnessing every day, the abuse of power that go unchecked by our leaders and the inequity that the pandemic has exacerbated. I was overwhelmed — trying to take in the ever-extreme range of this roller coaster of feelings. I was at the tiniest edge of just shutting down.

I was uncomfortable with these waves of rage I was experiencing. *I almost didn't recognize myself.* And as much as I was terrified and wanted to shut down, I looked towards that rage.

In this darkness was a glimmer; the jagged ends of my grief and exhaustion offering a glimmer of truth: **this moment was making me more radical.** I didn't say it out loud, but I saw it and I felt it. There was a truth sitting at the edges of my overwhelm, patiently waiting for me to see it.

To get to a place of new truth-telling, edgewalking, and embracing the radical, I had to lean in and not shrink. I had to expand to hold *all of the feelings*, holding in the pain and rage while also being able to function and be purposeful. This means showing up and doing my job while still being able to take care of myself while letting go of the shame that was not mine.

Rage has shown up many times in my life, even when I didn't know how to name it.

I've visited an immigration court in San Diego and watched the proceedings of asylum seekers brought into a courtroom with no interpreters, wearing ankle and wrist chains.

I've been at the border wall watching border patrol dehumanize the most vulnerable among us.

I've attended the funerals of young Black men killed by police.

I've observed policymakers make budget decisions with little regard for the humans affected.

I've listened to folks in philanthropy tell me how much they love humanity while they guard massive wealth from communities who are in such deep need.

And so many more moments where rage came to the surface.

I know this rage is me bearing witness fully and teaching me that I am able to be here for what is purposeful.

Reflect

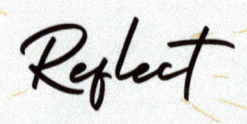

The practice of deep breathing coupled with strategizing and conspiring have supported me the most in my rage journey.

Take a deep breath, the kind that makes your whole body expand and get bigger.

Take up more space with your rage, and with this fresh breath, move towards love. Set an intention to let the rage you feel transform you, your actions and your vision of what is possible.

How can you channel your rage into action, big or small? How can you release rage as a demonstration of solidarity and love?

WHEN THE HURRICANE OF WHITENESS AND OPPRESSION BEARS DOWN, WE MIGHT GET RUFFLED AND SHAKEN.

LET'S NOT BE UPROOTED. NOURISH YOUR ROOTS TO GO DEEPER INTO YOUR PURPOSE.

KEEP GOING.

On Why It Hurts

We experience harm in so many ways within systems of oppression, white supremacy, patriarchy, and colonization. The Fuckery hides itself under the guise of normalcy, as if harm within the system is also normal.

Exhaustion and Burnout

There are lots of tired folks out here. So many of us are exhausted by the ongoing racism, bias, diminishment, and marginalization of our very being. We are tired of being the ones to always say something. We are tired of being the holders of this work, the consciousness keepers. We are tired in a multiplicity of ways. Sometimes, our own colleagues and networks exhaust us — family members too — with their stubborn and willful ignorance or unwillingness to engage in this work at any level.

The exhaustion isn't just physical tiredness or intellectual tiredness. By exhaustion, I mean the labor it takes to navigate the slowness, aggression, and the inevitable burnout. This is all holistically exhausting to our spirit, intellect, and emotions.

Burnout can be understood as the persistent and accumulating form of exhaustion and pressure taking its toll on us - the exploitation of our purpose and agency being extracted at a rate we cannot nourish or replenish.

We experience burnout in different ways and it can take a long time and effort (and privilege not all of us have) to recover and heal from it. It can take a lot of effort and time to heal from burnout.[1] From personal experience, my burnout journey has been a long one, at times painful, at times confusing, almost always requiring energy I couldn't seem to muster to do the honest exploration required around my healing, grief, purpose, and agency. It was a combination of dealing with the loss of my sweet dad, work, and personal things. Finally, 5 years into the journey, I feel like I am experiencing some ease and reconnecting with a deeper sense of my purpose.

Disconnection and Dehumanization

The Fuckery is a bully. It pushes us and taunts us into thinking that if we don't grind harder, we are going to lose. We get so busy and burnt out that we forget to be in our bodies. This blinds us to the undercurrents of what is really happening because we are on autopilot/survival mode, experiencing disconnection. We become disconnected from ourselves, our breath, our purpose, each other, and our communities.

In the worst of disconnection, we dehumanize ourselves and each other. A primary condition of systems of oppression functioning over time is to dehumanize; removing elements of joy, relationship, love, identity, experiences, and differences such that the outcome is that we can't see human beings anymore.

Disconnection and dehumanization break our bonds and fracture our shared power.

---

[1] To me, burnout means when both our purpose and our agency is broken. When the spark is extinguished and we see our agency only as limited and ineffective. And so, we wither.

Overwhelm and Hyperactivism

The ongoing designed chaos of systemic oppression pushes us to go harder and do all the things. This volume and pace of work create harm and overwhelm us. As a result, we can often disconnect altogether – and forget our agency. Importantly, this is also a process of coping within systems of oppression, with the unfortunate result being the same – disconnection, harm, and paralysis.

In response, many of us move into hyperactivism mode, which is a trauma response to the chaos. The feeling that I have to be vigilant, I have to fix it, I have to do more, I can't stop.[2] We don't have to be "on" all the time, but we do need to stay present and in our own humanity.

Shame

Many of us have experienced shame. In this work of changing the world away from The Fuckery, shame is nuanced and experienced in a multiplicity of ways from different root causes. Everyone experiences shame differently.

For those of us who have been given racialized and marginalized identities, shame was often put on us for just being who we are or for being boxed into stereotypes we cannot escape. Shame is a poison given to us to force conformity and silence.

White and racialized folks alike might also feel shame as a form of retaliation when we speak up to change the status quo, another way of not conforming and just accepting that it is what it is.[3]

---

[2] In contrast, another trauma response is paralysis, or even fully leaving one's world-changing work behind, which is as harmful as hyperactivism when it is the trauma's response to oppression.

[3] Often, for folks who are racialized and marginalized, this comes with a narrative telling us that while it is what it is, we should also just be grateful to even get to be here.

We might also feel shame because we have failed to show up as changemakers at a moment when we should have (and sometimes, moments where we wish we could have but couldn't). There is never a perfect way to do this work. Shame is a hallmark of creating paralysis in systems of oppression. It takes us out of our purpose and agency.

Remember, the shame white supremacy wants you to feel is not real. It is not yours to carry.

Consider different ways to interrupt the status quo so it is not always a burden but is instead an act of purpose. Acknowledge that this is hard and that some days won't be your day for this kind of work. That's ok. Also, remember that some people will choose conflict and confrontation no matter what you say or how you approach them. Choose your wellness and safety first. It is also okay to say what you need to say and leave. You don't have to be engaged if it hurts your humanity.

I can't breathe

Eric Garner
Javier Ambler
Manuel Ellis
Elijah McClain
George Floyd
Eleanor Northington
Alesia Thomas
Zachary BearHeels
Irvo Otieno
Chantal Moore
Eishia Hudson

There are so many more. So many lives taken from us.

We've heard the phrase "I can't breathe" multiple times, but even hearing it once is too much. The pattern tells us a story about sustained oppression.

As witnesses, our own breath becomes a sign of resistance, a long exhalation of rage and sorrow.

As activists and allies, our breath becomes our battle cry. The force that literally helps us tell the truth.

As beings, our breath is proof of being here – it is our humanity.

Pause

Rest.

Right now. Rest your head on your desk or sink back into the pillow. Lay down if you can. Nothing else. Just the simplest form of rest — a pause.

Remember, you matter and you are loved.

Strategic Compliance

Conform. Abide. Acquiesce. Submit. Cooperate. Yield. Comply. Oblige. Consent. Silence. Collude.

We are constantly navigating a system that forces compliance and asks us to work in ways that uphold comfort[1] and inequities. Most often, we are granted space to make a choice between 2 options: terrible and worse. We work with rules, plans, and strategies that do not offer benefits to the whole of the collective. We are asked to do this with gracefulness and politeness, honoring the fragility and so-called "starting points" of others. We are asked to navigate all of this while somehow maintaining our own well-being, health, financial stability, job security, and relationships. The underlying dynamic here is maintaining the comfort and stability of those in power and compliance.

Our identities play a large role in when and how we disrupt or when we are forced to comply strategically. For people who experience the world as racialized and marginalized, we often comply so we can survive. We comply to hold on to the space we've fought so hard for so that our vision and voice are not erased. Because without our voices, the powers that be won't be able to even see a different future. **We strategize not to comply but to stay.**

For those of us with privilege (which, of course, intersects with some who are also being racialized and marginalized), our compliance requires us to reflect on why we are complying; who and what

---

1 Comfort-keeping: the obligation (and demand) in systems of oppression to maintain the status quo rules by not being disruptive or impolite and not making others uncomfortable at the expense of the truth and experience of people who experience marginalization and racialization.

are we protecting? For individuals who hold significant privilege, compliance is a way to protect oneself and one's positionality within the community of the privileged.

Navigating risks while showing up is not a singular set of steps or rules. It changes with context, time, and what our hearts tell us we are willing/can risk. Risk is contextualized. It matters who we are when we are navigating the complexity of compliance. Racialized and marginalized people bear risks that are not experienced by those who have more privilege.

Among the most challenging ways we are asked to maintain comfort and stability is through comfort keeping — the ask of meeting the demands of the status quo by maintaining movement that never says the quiet part out loud; that never disrupts. We are asked to design our work within the parameters of what is palpable to those in power while also not implicating or indicting them as part of the problem. When we disrupt the status quo, we interrupt the normalized flow of whiteness, patriarchy, and othering. Being a disruptor comes with consequences ranging from subtle sighs of annoyance to extreme forms of retaliation and harm. When we speak up, ask questions, and take action to spark change, we weigh the risks to ourselves with the risks of not taking action or speaking up. It's never a fair equation and we know this daily navigation takes emotional, intellectual, and physical labor.

What does this all mean? It means we make choices. We are navigating a never-static set of conditions about risks, punishments and consequences, and privileges. Even when we want to (literally) say the quiet part out loud and take action, the choices we face come with risks. We are always navigating — both explicitly and implicitly — when, where and how we will disrupt or comply.

Being strategic

Complying requires us to acknowledge that we know the better thing to do while at the same time realizing that the risks of those actions can, at times, be too great, so we need to strategize.

Maybe our short-term actions to disrupt will compromise other long-term goals. Maybe we are burned out. Or maybe we sense that if we disrupt, we may put ourselves or others in danger. Making a choice to step back includes us considering and protecting ourselves, our families, and our livelihoods.

Compliance can cause us to question our agency, efficacy, and leadership. For some, it can bring up feelings of doubt, shame, unworthiness, and imposter syndrome.

It feels awful. This demand to conform leaves us feeling untethered and at odds with our own values.

Because it is.

But there is more to this than sitting with our perceived shortcomings of activism or courageousness. You need to remember that even in the worst of cases, forced compliance still has space for us to honor our own humanity and our own needs. We still have agency, even when we walk away, to instead invest in relationship building, or healing, or visioning.

We have to be strategic when we comply or disrupt because the goal is to show up another day to build together. I hope that regardless of the circumstances, you can always see space for you to choose how you show up.

We are navigating a series of elements to decide our course of action - often in the blink of an eye. In real time, we are considering: what choices are available to me given the dynamics of this moment?

Privilege

Privilege is a systemically informed resource that gives us access to authority, access to resources, space to make choices, the ability to influence, and the ability to protect or harm. How does having privilege influence your ability to create change?

Social location

Our many forms of identities inform our privilege and the role they play in navigating risks - both in the moment and long term. These identities come with varying levels of privilege and oppression.

Purposefulness

How clear and rooted are we in who we are in service to, and who we are in a relationship with?

Risk

The danger, losses, and retaliation that we are willing to bear in order to resist compliance and disrupt the status quo. What is at risk if I take a certain action? Are there other actions that mitigate the risk? What are the risks if I don't take action?

Power

What access to resources and authority do we have? Power is a capacity. How are we acknowledging our own power and mobilizing it?

Community and allies

Are we on our own? Where are our people? Who is there to link arms with us?

Often, we comply. We have to, given the navigation of the choices we are considering. If and when we stop at this point of compliance, it becomes complicitness.

However, if we pause to strategize, weighing all of the above choice points, we can strategically weigh the choices we still have, even if we have to comply in some ways, knowing we can still influence future outcomes. We do this by continuing to make choices that create space and momentum. We have options and pathways.

Embodiment to be Present
Taking a deep breath to stay present and connected.

Practicing Care
Investing in healing and taking care of ourselves and others in the collective so that we can come back again.

Movement Building
Connecting and mobilizing with fellow changemakers to move together and mobilize collective power.

Conspiring
Strategizing to uncover other pathways to influence change; planning for next time and moving allies into more active roles.

Designing Preconditions
Mitigating risk by addressing the real current conditions and starting where we are in order to protect oneself and the collective as best as possible – while also creating an opening or shift for change in the longer term.

Reflect

On disruption
1. What risks might I face in disrupting, and am I willing to take these risks?
2. What mitigation strategies do I need to move forward? Might I be able to set myself up for more success?
3. Who benefits from my disruption?
4. Does this disruption of the status quo create space for creating collective good?
5. Are there intermediate or incremental steps I can take to mitigate the consequences?
6. Who are my allies, and can I call them in?

Reflect

On forced compliance
1. Go back to a time when you complied with the system.
2. Can you see yourself as human in that instance?
3. Why am I complying? (bring awareness, not judgment).
4. What are other areas in which I can be and feel like I am contributing purposeful labor?

49

Reflect

On strategic compliance
1. How can I take care of myself today?
2. What are my plans for coming back strong the next time?
3. How am I going to continue to be present and purposeful in my labor? How can I uplift my agency even when asked to yield? How will I choose to be subversive and strategic?

we're going in a different direction...

breathe

This is a moment to turn ourselves towards what we are creating and building. Let's take a moment to ready ourselves.

Rest this book down for a moment and bring your attention to your breathing.

Take a gentle breath in.

Gently, gently, gently.

No need to force a deep breath. Take it slow. Breathe in and out slowly until you find yourself centering a gentle breathing pattern.

What do you feel?

Do you feel the temperature of the air moving through your nose?

This is the reminder that you are here, in this place, present in this specific moment.

Take another breath in slowly.

Gently breathe in and then let out a slow exhale.

What do you feel?

Is your rib cage expanding? Is your body posture changing?

This is the reminder that you are here, in your body.

Try a deeper breath now, intentionally expanding your lungs, rib cage, and belly. Bring that breath deep into your body.

This is a reminder of your gifts and your beautiful self occupying an essential and needed space in this world.

Rooted in Purpose

May we find pathways to define our labor as meaningful and heart-filling.

Purpose

Your purposefulness matters to all of us.

There is a lot to be done in the world. It can be overwhelming.

Purpose is rooted in contribution and is what helps us keep going.[1]

One of the biggest lies of The Fuckery is that we have to do it all, accepting burnout and exploitation as changemakers. I find reflecting on my purpose helpful. Instead of looking for passion or "self-care," reflecting on our purpose helps us stay rooted in collective service, defining our own meaningful labor and giving us space to show up again and again. We can activate the power we hold — that each of us individually holds.

Purpose recenters our actions and labor on what matters — how we be (as in being) within the collective. Remember, **purpose is the antidote to overwhelm and fear**. With what capacity we have, let's recenter on what matters for the collective. We have limited time, energy, power, and money. Purpose helps us sharpen how we contribute within the collective — it directs our voice and amplifies it. You know what it feels like to be out of your purpose — it's draining and frustrating, leaving you feeling pulled in too many directions. Purpose creates focus.

When we put purpose first, speaking the truth feels powerful instead of causing anxiety or paralysis. Purpose first allows us to get up every day in a world that can often feel overwhelming, harsh, and intimidating — and in spite of that, we still love, connect, and

---

[1] It is the thing that even when The Fuckery shows up in its full Fuckery, you still show up because it matters - to you and to us.

take care of ourselves and each other.

It's amazing how being in one's purpose is also energy-giving. Energy spent on meaningful contributions within the collective — within relationships — can be exhausting. However, this exhaustion lives side by side with the soul-nourishment of purpose as well. Purpose is what allows us to keep on keeping on. It is where big, unfearing vision and belief in the possible thrive.

Purpose lives in you — you feel it in your bones. You know that silence or bystanding or small thinking is simply not an option when you know that people — your fellow humans — need you to do better.

Once you find your purpose, commit to being there with all you have.

P.S. You choose how you live in your purpose. This work will always beckon, and be hard and scary. And if it becomes apparent to you that the labor you are offering is not meaningful, you can choose a different path. I want you to live on your terms, through your own choices. Do not let The Fuckery choose for you.

Reflect

Purpose changes over time. Take a few moments to reflect deeply on your purpose.

Find some quiet time, perhaps outside in a park or in your favorite nook in your home.

On the following journal pages and with your pens and crayons, take some time to complete this reflection.

On the first page, write or draw your response to: What am I compelled to contribute to this work that feels meaningful? What feels meaningful for my labor?

"This work" could mean a project or career path. Or it could mean the big-picture view of changing the world for the collective good.

Don't judge or edit the words as they come. Allow the words to flow. If you get stuck, pause and let your mind and heart wander. Then come back and add any other ideas that come to you.

Sometimes, at the top of this list, there are actions that feel like they may have been given to you — through a job description, for example. Keep going and see what comes up for you - from you. You might be surprised.

Circle the few that resonate with you. Focus on the ones you would wake up happily for, even if challenging. Of those on the list, what do you want to reclaim through your purpose?

After doing this first reflection, take a second piece of paper and continue: In order to be of service to those things that feel most purposeful, what do I have to let go of?

Consider what you might believe about your role. What ideas have others given to you about your work? Consider what you can let go of in order to be more fully present for your purpose.

And as a third step on another piece of paper, draw or write a response to the questions: what is the energy I want to emanate? What is my vibe when I am in the flow of my purpose?

Reflect

What am I compelled to contribute to this work that feels meaningful? What feels meaningful for my labor?

Reflect

In order to be of service to those things that feel most purposeful, what do I have to let go of?

Reflect

What do I want to emanate? What is my vibe when I am in the flow of my purpose?

Letting Go

Over many years of doing the Rooted in Purpose reflection, I've been able to evolve and grow new pathways for my labor and voice to show up. It's helped me stay rooted even when all I wanted to do was leave and become a professional potter (or surfer or roadway median gardener).

I've had so many important learnings over the years about what is purposeful — here are two that I come back to again and again:

First: it's not all my work. In order to stay in my purpose (to center Black, Indigenous, and People of Colors[1]) and speak truth, I've had to let go of certain kinds of work that are not mine to do, even if I deeply care about it. This includes letting go of having to become a practitioner and advocate of all things and instead engage in what supports my mission-focused work.

It also led me to an important learning: I had to let go of managing the tears of white women who weaponize their hurt. I had to realize that it is not about me. When I was younger, I was taught to keep the peace, assimilating into white dominant culture by being obedient. It's been challenging to release this sense of guilt — that somehow, because I've told the truth about oppression, it's my fault white women feel a certain way and are upset.

---

[1] I use People of Many Colors because I am trying to break up the monolithic idea of color and trying to both humanize us and to give us some space and nuance within the POC and BIPOC terms. It's to unerase us and let us all be seen. More often, I use the language of people who are racialized and marginalized to implicate systems of racialization and marginalization, and also create space for intersectional identities to be seen.

I've learned that I am purposeful in this work when I create spaces that support healing among racialized and marginalized people and their authentic allies.

Second: I can't force people into being better humans. My intellectual self knows this, but I struggled with seeing folks who are unwilling to try. I internalized it as my failure. I struggled when folks I work with failed over and over again to show up. I would feel guilt and defeat at the end of long days of staff workshops when the response to the last reflection was, "This was interesting, but I don't think the problems are as bad as you say it is. We've come a long way."

My purpose is to tell the truth in a way that lets people of color be seen and be safe, that centers them in our shared space and creates a culture of care for them, even in the most mundane meetings... Once I accepted this, a new world of work opened up for me.

I am able to go much deeper into finding my voice and my pathway when I remember these two truths. They allow me to show up more honestly and create space for more folks to engage in this work with me. They also help me make space for other people to activate their own agency and invest in creating a movement for the collective. Letting go makes more space for authentic work.

At the end of the day, I can rest, even if frustrated, knowing that I've done my meaningful labor.

Unencumbered

*Unentangled. Spacious. Free. Light. Stretchy. Flexible. Infinite. Flow. Decolonized. Multiplicity. Dynamic. Curious. Growth. Unbound*ed.

What happens when we stretch beyond being encumbered; when we move past the way that the world tells us to be?

What does it feel like to be unencumbered?

In unencumbering, we have space to create. We create space to release the burdens of assimilation and the ask to be a certain way, allowing us to express ourselves in our own self-determined way.

Being unencumbered is liberation — freedom from entanglements, should-haves and should-bes. It is the putting down of the weights that have been placed on us so that we can fully express who we are, not who the status quo says we should be. Liberation is the space to create, name, grow, and be in our bodies and community in the ways we choose. It is about the space to express and nourish one's self-determined identity, language, and intergenerational life vision in ways that are healing, and joyful, with access to all of the resources needed to bring that vision to life, and in a way that is met with love. This is especially true for those who have been marginalized and racialized.

This is what we are here to do. We are here to find this spaciousness and to grow into it in our own special ways, pushing off the pressures and bindings that limit us.

Reflect

First, let's take a moment to be fully present.

Close your eyes, relax in the space you are in, and feel the support of the ground beneath you.

Next, on a few sheets of sticky notes, write out some of the ways you carry the weight of being encumbered. Is it perfectionism, the "I have to do it all right now" feeling? Is it compliance, the need to be the "keep everyone comfortable" anchor? Is it the fear of very real risks, of anger or retaliation?

Write it all out, whatever the 'it' may be.

After you've written these notes, stick them on your body.

Really, stick them on yourself.

Reflect on what this feels like to be encumbered. You've named it. For a moment, let your body tap into and be aware of what it feels like to carry all these.

Slowly peel off the encumbrances one by one. Rip them up, stomp on them, crumple them up – burn them.

Reflect on what it feels like to release them, putting down what is not yours to carry.

Now, take a deep breath.

What does it feel like to drop these encumbrances and constraints?

Can you feel the possibility? Can you feel the infinite possibility of you? Of the collective?

Reflect

What are some of the things that hinder your inner changemaker?

Reflect

What are you afraid of losing or confronting?

Reflect

What are ways you can remind yourself to be intentional about unencumbering?

Agency

Sometimes we wait for permission to do the work.

We know what we see out there — we know because we bear witness and we feel that rage, grief, kinship, motivation, and love.

Often when we bear witness, there is a pause — sometimes subtle and sometimes explicit. We are waiting for permission. We wait while we labor in the work of convincing others to take action, for bosses, people, families, etc. We wait for permission to do the things we know are necessary.

Enough.

The opportunity to take action is often more present than we think. Consider in the space you occupy what you can do today. Consider what you can do right now. You already have the agency to make a choice.

Can you change all the things? No.

Can you change something that matters to the collective? 100% yes.

Live into your agency.

Reflect

Where have you assumed permission is needed before you can act?

Reflect

What do you bear witness to that compels you to action?

Reflect

What can you give yourself permission to do?

HOPE IS NOT A PRECONDITION TO ACTION.

• • • • • • • • • • • • • •

YOUR AGENCY IS THE MANIFESTATION OF HOPE.

Presence

Your breath brings you into presence. You cannot be present without your breath.

It is essential to our work that we remember to be here, not in the to-do lists, the busyness, and the grind. Here in the current moment. We have to reclaim our presence in this world.

Taking a few deep breaths, even for a few moments, is one of the most powerful ways to reclaim your space here.

Being away from our breath is a form of unbeing. Connecting with your breath is an act of liberation.

We've been taught to disconnect and work on autopilot. The status quo has pushed busyness and hustle over presence and connection. We become workers of the status quo, moving through the world disconnectedly, sometimes not even remembering our own bodies. And while breathwork is not the antidote to systemic forms of oppression, it is essential so we can self-determine how we will show up, navigate, and be present. Breath helps us own our own space, our own agency.

The biggest danger in forgetting our breath and our presence in the moment is losing the opportunity to show up fully embodied as a changemaker, and losing the choice of how we will be responsible in this moment. In the day-to-day grind of our lives and work, we sometimes disconnect from our breath. It keeps on keepin' on, even if we pay no attention to it.

The status quo moves through us effortlessly when we become inattentive to being present. In that stress (burnout, inattentiveness) comes the danger. The danger that we will hurt ourselves and each other, overlooking opportunities to be purposeful and of service, forgetting the big vision. Our vision and labor become clouded when we are unaware of and disconnected from our breath.[1]

This reflection on breath is an invitation to reconnect — to liberate ourselves from the spaces that tell us to forget ourselves and instead just go; the spaces and work that tell us to produce more, to do more, to be more, and to do all that with less. We are told to do all this with less time, less wellness, less connection, less resources, and less love.

When we stay aware of and are intentional with our breathing, we allow ourselves to show up in the world. Our breath reminds us to pause the rapid-fire nature of the status quo and to choose a different flow. We need to be our full selves in order to tackle the work ahead.

Breathwork is usually associated with the concept of mindfulness. The word *mindfulness*[2] comes from the Buddhist word sati, which means to remember, being aware. I'd like to offer that we start with

---

1 In colonized and commodified spaces, self-care, breathwork, and mindfulness have become hyper-individualized and self-centered. When we become unencumbered from these notions of westernized wellness, our breath is the first step to reclaiming relationships; being present and connected in our community and remembering that we are interconnected. When we move past ourselves and our hyper-individualized embodiment, our breath brings us into relationship, community, and service with ourselves and each other.

2 I don't think that mindfulness is the best word to use. It tends to reinforce hyper-intellectualization and analysis of our worldly experiences. Remembering who we are is the work of our heart space, of connection with one another in most of the important ways - remembering our humanity. Research tells us that ancient Buddhist texts that used the word sati were translated in the 19th century as the word mindfulness by T. W. Rhys Davids (a British magistrate), and continued to be adopted as these practices were moved into the Western world. Also remember, this was at the height of the British global colonization.

a recognition that this is very likely not the work of the mind or even thought. It is presencing: the embodied openness of our heart and spirit to remember our shared humanity without judgment.

If we are unencumbered and embodied, we are able to remember that we are here, in this moment, in this body, and in this space.

Remembrance is not about just being present for ourselves. We are not here to be well only for ourselves. We are here to show up for ourselves and each other with presence, honor, love, and growth. As folks who are committed with our whole being to change the world, we know our work is for ourselves when it is also for one another.

Liberating your inner changemaker starts with letting yourself breathe.

Liberating your inner changemaker starts with letting yourself breathe.

Healing

One way to understand healing is to see it as a sense of spaciousness beyond the sharp edges of hurt, trauma, and pain. It is the space for our experiences to co-exist without the pain blanketing or defining our wellness and joy; the space for each of us to traverse our own paths beyond the limits of what pain defines. Healing means trauma can exist without being the sustained and prevailing condition of who and how we are in the world.

When we carry a lot - which we do - we might feel squeezed as if we are walking in a narrow and too-small tunnel, as if the space around us to take a deep breath or stretch our arms out is getting smaller and smaller.

When we intentionally put labor into our own and collective healing, spaciousness makes itself present. Literally, we create time in our calendars, we create space in our spirit to consider what might bring us some ease and wellness.

Healing in this way also invites us into a deeper connection with our full selves. The practices of healing, specific to each of us and emergent in our journeys, are about coming into a closer connection with ourselves, which we cannot do when trauma and hurt are taking up all the space. It is not about "fixing" but instead making space for healing focused on growth and grounded in safety, gentleness, and time.

It is an ongoing practice to invest time and labor into yourself. Healing is not necessarily easy or straightforward. It is not a one-time self-care massage session, a weekend wellness retreat, or a DEI session at work. While those may be helpful, healing work happens when we establish practices to regularly tend to our wounds, exhaustion, and burnout while investing in experiencing joy, love, and spirit. It is in breaking through patterns that keep us from growing into our full selves and that are practices situated in communal connection.

Healing practices are as individual as each of you. Find what works to help you breathe more deeply, experience joy more fully, and feel more nourished and connected. Healing goes at your pace when you are ready. No one else can heal for you or push you to heal. When you are ready, tend to the hurt and wounds, reach out for support, call in your community.

Caring for ourselves is a practice of collective care; healing work is collective as well. Sometimes we might forget that indeed, each of us is in the collective - our own presence creates the collective. Our own wellness and healing work lights a path for others to see that it is possible. It gives permission for others to do this work.

Reflect

We are the pathmakers, the edgewalkers, the changemakers, the radicals, the activists, the healers and the doers, the risk takers, and the big vision holders.

What do you need to feel more ready, nourished, and stronger as you take the next step in this journey?

What can you tend to and soothe?

Where can you find spaciousness in your spirit? What might or does it feel like to have spaciousness for your body to breathe deeply?

John Chief Moon

In October 2019, I was in Mohkinstsis (the Blackfoot name for Calgary, Alberta, Canada, Treaty 7 Territory), visiting the Tsuut'ina Nation to lead a workshop on racial equity for an audience of about 50 community, nonprofit, and philanthropic leaders.

Honestly, I was nervous. I remember thinking, "How am I going to share offerings to the originators of this work? On their land?" I was feeling unsure.

Taking a deep breath, I jumped up on the little stage in front of flip charts and the screen. It was a beautiful, fun, and laughter-filled day as we talked communally about inclusion, race, and equity. I remember looking out at so many faces, wishing I understood more about what was actually happening out in the crowd while I facilitated – was my presentation making sense for their lives and context?

At the end of the day, we spent some time listening to closing remarks from the attendees. It was moving to hear that it was a meaningful and purposeful day.

After a few folks spoke, a tall man stood up. I remember bracing myself, feeling unsure about what he might say. His gravitas reached all the way across the room. His name was John Chief Moon.[1]

---

1   This story is shared with permission from John Chief Moon. John Chief Moon is a Knowledge Keeper from the Kainai Nation (Blood Tribe) in Alberta, Canada. In an article in Windspeaker Magazine, he is quoted as saying "If I can say something or do something and it can help even one person, it's worth it. I'm not naïve. I'm not going to undo 500 years of colonialism. But if I can teach one person at a time, it's helpful."

In a gentle and firm voice, he shared that Blackfoot people are known for their strong warriors and that he himself comes from a lineage of warriors. Warriors are people who did and do the hard thing or the brave thing to protect others and for their community. Looking right at me he said, "Bina, she is also a warrior because she also does that. She is doing the hard work — what needs to be done — and she doesn't stop when it's hard."

My heart broke open. Being purposeful — even when uncertain or nervous — helps you earn your allyship. More than that, it shows that we can do this work differently, in ways that heal and do not harm. We can do it together.

After the session, he and I got to speak more in-depth; it remains one of the most impactful days of my life. I realized I was being seen in this work and that I could also be part of the story in a room of the most amazing community.

When you show up fully, honestly, and with purpose, you earn your space as an ally. And when we are in community together, the most amazing gift is to let other folks know this.

I am forever grateful for that day with John Chief Moon and his reassurance.

I am grateful to have been seen and to know that I am a warrior because I am purposeful in the work, not because I perform it.

I invite you to reconnect with your inner warrior too. ***It is in there. Let others see it too.***

Reflect

Remember a time in which you felt seen. How did it feel?

Reflect

How do you nourish your inner warrior?

Reflect

How does your labor show up as love?

Reflect

What rules will you break?

Nothing is unchangeable. Systems of oppression are intentionally designed.

This means we can undesign them[1]

---

[1] As ugly and horrific as oppression, the system offers a spark of opportunity - and us as changemakers seizing it is the beauty within the horror.

Jalebi and Hard Truths

I was seven years old when my parents decided to go to Mumbai for a long holiday to see our family. It was a three-month trip, which meant missing a lot of school. My teacher had even sent along a *literal* suitcase worth of homework, which I was required to do daily before going out to play or explore.

Sitting at the giant table in my grandparent's dining room — the same table my father sat at as a child doing his homework — I resentfully traced my hand into a misshapen turkey. I know the resentment was about doing homework while on holiday (obviously), but now, I know it was also about having to deal with the multiple levels of cross-continental colonization it symbolized. It really is that inescapable: *colonization*.

And it wasn't lost on me as a child, even if I couldn't name it. Growing up as the first-generation daughter of immigrants in the United States, I had already spent the entirety of my life navigating spaces that were meant for others — never for people like me — where the norms and practices didn't account for me and my family or background, but only that of the colonizer.

I remember sighing deeply, staring out a colorfully patterned window into the garden, Diwali paper lanterns and flowers floating in the hot, sticky breeze. I snuck a mischievous look at my dad, and we quietly tucked my assignment away into a folder to be forgotten and piled into our beloved old Ambassador for an adventure.

***

My mother and sisters had gone into a shop to look through a stack of silky patterned saris. Standing outside the alley, people-watching and eating street sweets, my dad and I were in our own happy place.

Every detail of this moment is still etched in my mind. As we sat there, I looked across the road and saw a young boy about my age. We looked like we could have known each other on the playground. As we stared at each other, him crouched under the train platform peering out and me staring back, eating warm, sticky jalebi from the street vendor, I wondered if he had ever had to make a hand turkey.

But then, something caught my eye.

I turned to my dad as I watched him and whispered, "Why is his hair orange?"

We were the same, yet I knew we were not. My young brain tried to figure it out. His hair looked more like the color of the jalebi, sticking out at all angles like straw. I'd never seen anything like it before.

In his gentle voice, my dad said, "Well, he doesn't have enough good food to eat, and his hair can't grow like yours. All those vitamins and good food you get make your hair black, your eyes see clearly, and your bones strong."

"But don't his parents feed him?" I asked, puzzled.

"Well, *Beta*, they probably don't have much money and can't get the food they need."

"Someone can help them. Right? Who can bring them food?" I pushed, my voice both defiant and trembling.

My sweet dad looked at me, knowing I was too young to fully understand but old enough to hold this unfathomable reality. I remember him saying, "There really isn't anyone, but he'll be okay. He'll be okay."

Then we got up and walked into the store to find my mom and

sisters and carried on with our day.

Decades later, I still think of this moment often. It is one of those memories that burrowed its way into my long-term memory and being. It changed my bones and the tempo of my heartbeat. That moment changed me forever and taught me a fundamental truth that I would live by.

There can never be no one.

Reflect

Think back to a moment that taught you a hard truth, changed your understanding of the world, and brought you to your work.

Share your story — write it out here, say it out loud, and let it weep onto these pages if it needs to.

WHEN THE CALL TO ACTION IS MIGHTY, REFUSE A SMALL VISION.

LIBERATION LIVES IN YOUR BIG VISION.

Onwards, Together

Together is our only way to a better future.

Find Your People

We are kin.

Our work is to find our people, to connect to one another, share in the labor, and trust that each of us will hold it down. Purpose is collective.

We are here to see each other and build a movement. Collective change comes through organizing (finding and connecting with your people) and advocacy (being seen and saying the quiet part out loud).

We need to invest in ourselves and in our fellow travelers up this mountain. Invest time, love, money, rest, and connection in yourself and other folks willing to reimagine and do the work.

It's not up to one of us to do this work — it is up to each of us.

Imagine the possibility...

Rest

Rest and replenishment are part of anti-oppression work — an essential component to unleash our creative agency and undo the forces of capitalism and exploitation. Disrupting the status quo includes rest, joy, love, and naps. Importantly, like breathwork, rest allows us to reconnect with our agency and to have the capacity to show up in our deepest purpose.

We need rest and healing. We are not meant to be "activist enough" or operate on level 10 all the time, 24/7. Burnout — literally the light going out, the voice being silenced — is not the request. The request of liberation is first to be well in this work so that we can be together in this work today and tomorrow. Rest is a resource that can guide our ability to connect, be creative, let our imaginations be free and nourished to see the future, to simply be who we are.

There is so much excellent care being taken around this topic of rest. Take time to learn from others laying out pathways for us.

Rest. Without explanation or guilt.

Rest because you — beautiful human — are here.

Pause

Rest is essential to changing the world. We are not meant to burn out (be exploited beyond return) in our work as edgewalkers, game changers, Elders, and revolutionaries.

Take a moment to pause.

Just sit. Slump down a little bit so your body can rest while the sofa does its work. Sink into an easeful space.

Close your eyes ever so gently.

And now is the perfect moment to take a nap.

Rest. The work will be here when you come back.

Commit to rest on your calendars. Block time out. Make it real. Rest is a part of this work. Prioritize it. Nourish it. Protect it.

The Mountain

I'll share an analogy that helps me frame my work: *The Mountain*.

So many of us are standing at the trailhead, which is the start of a pathway leading up the side of a tall mountain. We feel ready. Some folks have gone before us, and we can hear their echoes and see their outlines disappearing into the distance.

The work to climb the mountain (the real work of anti-oppression, racial justice, and liberation) is immense and challenging. It requires effort and multi-racial, multi-ethnic, intergenerational, gender-inclusive, and anti-ableist healing and relationship building.

There are those of us who put effort into unencumbering from what oppression and colonization have taught us, from what society, our parents, pastors and priests, communities, and social life have taught us about ourselves and each other.

For those climbing, we are willing to shed comfort to learn how to be in a new relationship with each other and the earth. We don't know what the pathway up the mountain holds, but we are laced up and ready to try. Backpacks ready, eyes turned upwards, machetes ready to clear the pathway — we are in this together.

So why *The Mountain?* While the paths and trek may be unknown to us, they have been walked before. Our ancestors have walked them. They have mapped and cleared these paths before. Some of the paths may be overgrown, and we need to clear them. Some may no longer serve us, so we become the ones who will trek a new way forward for those who come after.

We also do not need to know the view at the top of the summit to know this trek is necessary and that there is a view — a gorgeous view. We know that there is a horizon waiting for us. We know.

There is joy, healing, creativity, and community in this trek. Ask any hiker, and they may tell you it is hard, but each step is meaningful. This is where the work is: reimaging what is possible and then building towards this new possible. As we hike, we may imagine and dream of the views — the fresh open air, the resting places under the clouds at the top of the mountain, the feel of soil and roots under our feet.

As a collective of climbers — *the collective* — we offer different gifts and strengths that support the whole in a multitude of ways. Some of us leave cairns, some walk with machetes to clear the path, and some walk behind to yell encouragement and make sure no one gets left behind. And it is in this collective climb that, in our own ways, we each can say the quiet part out loud.

The journey offers space to give and receive. It is a reminder that it is not on one of us to do this work alone. Our journey to liberation and freedom is interconnected — we must (re)connect with ourselves and each other.

Something interesting happens as we assemble at the trailhead when we get ready to climb. Some of us get a tap on the shoulder.

"But what about me? Can you hold my backpack?"

"I really want to see the view but don't want to hike — can we drive to the top?"

"Tie my shoes, get me water. You told me it was a walk, not a hike...."

One of the hardest parts of this work is that when many of us are at the trailhead — some of us are already climbing — there are stragglers and naysayers. Their unrelenting distractions take us away from our purpose: wellness, creating, building, climbing, and connecting.

Behold, the "Parking Lot Gang." The ones who wander around, spending so much time trying to convince us that they want to hike without ever actually doing the work. Importantly, they are connected and organized. They are not individualized actors — there is also a communal element to their gang. Their misdirected labor is a distraction to us, and causes harm. You know them: the intellectualizers, the resistors, the bystanders, the performers, the leechers, the shortcutters, the pacers, and the disconnecters.[1]

---

1   Let's name them. And also note, there are even more folks out there who aren't named here - they are harmful and violent in so many ways.
The Intellectualizers: There are a variety of folks scattered about the parking lot. Some have backpacks but they won't stop reading the guidebook about the hike. They will tell you everything about the local fauna, they know the type of shoes to wear and how much the trek will cost you, but they won't walk to the trailhead yet (or ever). These are the folks stuck in the "preparing and being ready" cycle.
The Resistors: Others won't even get out of the car. These are our folks who may know about the mountain, but they are not going to hike it. These are also our folks who have seen a picture of a different mountain and feel like that informed them enough about all mountains. Sometimes, they try to lock us in the car with them.
The Bystanders: Some do get out of the car — wandering around the parking lot aimlessly but never directed towards the trailhead. These are the "taking it in" voyeurs who acknowledge the work ahead, but they don't want to do it. But they sure do like being adjacent enough to feel like they could do it.
The Performers: They want a bench to sit on and get the view — telling anyone who will listen about the mountain. They stretch, they have the best hiking gear and they know everyone who is anyone who has reached the summit. But these are our folks who never get dirty. These are our folks who will only act as far as it risks nothing.
The Leechers: Many say, "Ok — we'll go, but carry my stuff up, will you?" Those who want the glory at the top but want someone else to get them there and only in a way that makes them comfortable and keeps them in control — allowing them to set the conditions of the journey. They also might push you off the edge when you get to the top.
The Shortcutters: These are the folks who send a drone to the top and then send back out-of-context images and analyses that are then commercialized into a product. These are our toolkit people who believe that without even leaving their homes, they can call themselves mountain climbers.
The Pacers: Stuck in the fretting and shame of not knowing there was a mountain, of not

They are not the work. These folks who are aimlessly and willfully wandering away from the trailhead are not the work. Well, they are definitely not the work for all of us. Allies[2] : you are essential in meeting these folks where they are — this is your work as allies, to manage the parking lot gang so others can do the work of healing, connecting, climbing, and leading.

And so, we are here for the coalition of the willing. We are here to invest in each other, to be in a relationship. We are here for the collective. For us.

---

having the right shoes, of not knowing that their ancestors tried to bulldoze the mountain — these are our folks who have disengaged their agency and cannot move outside of the "I" narrative and handwringing.
The Disconnected: The ones who say mountains only exist in the past — these are our folks who live right next to mountains and they call them hills and even then — the earth is flat.

2   Allies come from a diverse range of race, ethnicity, gender, age, and other identities.

Reflect

We all get that tap on the shoulder, *Truth-asking* is a tool you can use to respond. It is impossible to get to a more truthful answer if the question is a lie. Asking questions to let other folks say their own quiet parts out loud is a powerful accountability tool. Asking questions also allows us to interrupt the behaviors of resistance without immediately creating aggressive confrontations.

What are more truthful questions you can ask? Here are a couple of ideas:

Can you say more about what you mean?

What, in your experience, makes you respond this way?

A simple question or a series of questions that are themselves rooted in liberation and anti-oppression are some of the greatest tools we can have. They open up space under the surface — getting us to the roots of an issue or problematic take.

The truth unfolds not only in the telling but when it is persuaded into the light by a more honest question.

Radical possibility is unencumbered vision, heart, and mindset change.

It is seeing another pathway forward and bringing others along to build.

That is how we change the world!

Radical Possibility

Your vision of a liberated future for us is the one thing that cannot be colonized.[1] It is yours to build from.

Radical possibility is unencumbered vision, heart and mindset change, seeing another pathway forward, and bringing others along to build. That is how we change the world.

The power sits in knowing there is another way to do life and imagining other ways of thriving, wellness, success, and being. There is a liberatory boldness to seeing this other way of being whole and well without the constraints of The Fuckery. It is a radical act to know and see that other pathways are possible in spite of the encumbrances that try to diminish our sight.[2]

After reclaiming our breath and reconnecting to our own purpose, unleashing our vision becomes a powerful practice, visualizing a world where we can abolish, defund, demilitarize, and be free. Can you see that world centered on love, community, joy, and self-determination?

Unbound and unencumbered. Your radical vision of what is possible is among the most beautiful space, free of compliance and complicity. It is yours.

This envisioning sparks action, allowing us to manifest a different way of showing up in the work of anti-oppression. Believing in the actualization of what is possible — beyond the encumbered place — allows us to heal and move forward simultaneously. We can design

---

1   A deep moment of gratitude to our ancestors, who taught us to hold onto a liberated vision of our own.
2   It feels good, doesn't it!

spaces to breathe, create, and build, going beyond simply imagining a different world to asking, "What is possible in this moment?"

This is the heart of radical possibility — that we can catalyze what we envision into our actions at this moment.

There is healing and power in the act of asking our imaginations, "Okay, and how? What can we do today to start bringing this vision to life? How do we create the future from where we are now? What are we moving towards?" We are meant to be builders and use our creative energy and talents to move away from the disrupting and yielding, away from the distractions of the parking lot gang, to instead *build a more beautiful today and tomorrow. This building, when centered on purpose, is a sustainable and sustained practice - the realm of possibility is not a moment in time. It is a practice.*

We must expand ways of knowing and learning beyond white dominant "expertise" and welcome alternative and new wisdom into colonized spaces by unerasing and uplifting voices that have been marginalized. We do this by expanding spaces of belonging through the voices, ideas, histories, and ways of knowing beyond those currently platformed and given power. Most importantly, we must ensure that people can self-determine how they want to participate in these spaces.

These practices, of envisioning, breathing, inviting in, and then building towards what is possible, are how we can do this work radically, joyfully, and unencumbered. We get so stuck in constrained and encumbered nonsense that we often don't build towards what is possible — in the grandest, most healing, and holistic way of understanding possibility.

Radical possibility is not about a latent imagination or hope. It is an active and willful rejection of the notion that because *it is does not mean it shall be.*

Invest in your vision of what is possible. Hold it close, even when the world tells you it just can't be. The time you've taken to craft this vision is a gift for all of us. It can change others when they hear your vision or observe you building toward it.

The future you radically envision is not for building tomorrow but is present *in this moment*.

LET'S START WITH WHAT IS NECESSARY, NOT WITH WHAT IS ALLOWED.

Reflect

What is your most radical vision of what is possible?

Gather a few supplies: crayons, colored pencils, or watercolors. Take a few minutes for each of the following words, and draw or paint what comes to you when you read the following words. If you are not a coloring person, map it in your own handwriting. Maybe say it out loud. It's not about being perfect or being an "artist" — just let it flow.

Reflect

How do you envision community?

Reflect

How do you reimagine power?

Reflect

How do you call on your ancestors?

Reflect

How will you manifest joy?

We Walk Together

I have so many stories of when I have called on my fellow edgewalkers, radicals, revolutionaries, and Elders in this work. I have, as I am sure you do, a long list of folks who have broken my heart and turned my brain inside out, showing me how much they don't want to change the world, that they don't care, that they are too afraid, that their proximity to power has dehumanized them.

Over and over again, I have found ways to remember that I walk with so many other people in this world who get it, people who understand what we are here to do. I know them in different ways, or know of them. I call them in a multitude of ways. I know — even in the hardest of moments — that I am always walking with a community of ancestors and relations.

You do too.

Reflect

Take a breath.

Turn your body so that your heart is centered on your people. Turn your heart away from the comfort-keeping demands of others and towards your purpose.

Physically make a shift and take a few deep breaths.

Remember what you are here to do, who you are here for, and who you are here with.

How does that feel? How does it feel to recenter within a circle of community, not just individually?

How does it feel to remember that we walk together?

Close your eyes and envision fellow warriors, abolitionists, advocates, and changemakers. Maybe you know them personally, maybe not.

Think of the artists and joy-makers who have shown you that love and joy are possible through their own forms of art, dance, and storytelling.

Bring to mind those folks who are making the world better.

Now picture yourself among them, standing shoulder to shoulder. Feel their energy, the warmth of their closeness. Visualize the group growing, and you standing among the growing community.

What are the qualities of these folks - your people?

How will you see, love on, and affirm your fellow changemakers?

How will you allow yourself to be seen and uplifted by them?

Keep Going

Thank you for all you do.

I see you. In a world that obscures the efforts of changemakers, edgewalkers and truth-tellers, I see you. I say this with my whole heart:

You've got this.

Be kind to yourself on this journey. Go step by step, without judgment, pouring generously into yourself and the collective.

I know **we** can do this; it is my deepest belief. I know we can change the world into one built by us for us. Our work is to unrelentingly build our movement together. That's the work that will change the world.

Go gently in your power...

How will you say the quiet part out loud?

Gratitude

Do you know what feels awesome? This moment of pause to reflect on the fantastical humans in my life. They make my heart bigger and nourish me - they show up for me. I hope you each know I am eternally grateful to be a part of your world and that you make mine better.

I am so deeply grateful for the many hearts that are open, the wisdom that is shared so lovingly, and the love and encouragement of so many as I carry on with my journey.

My husband Brandon: thank you for this life we are building together and for always keeping a cool head and warm heart. Who knew this is where we'd be?! Thank you for always believing in me, for your support and encouraging me. Even when I didn't see that it was possible, you did.

My dear parents, family in the U.S and India, my chosen family of friends near and far, colleagues, clients, co-conspirators, allies, Elders who are with us and ancestors who have left this earthly experience, your care, love, and teachings have changed me for the better. I'm grateful to be in community with you and be part of this shared arc of history. You teach me lessons about making the world more beautiful and how to move through the world with more grace. You've supported me and held space for me when I was feeling untethered and you have so deeply contributed to my understanding that, indeed, together, we can change the world. I am thrilled and full of joy that we are our people.

Truly, the work of bringing to life years of practice, words, ideas ... It doesn't happen alone. Marci of La Libertad Consulting: thank you for your thoughtful partnership, collaboration, and friendship. You have always shown up with love and truth, helping me stay in close fidelity to my work while also helping it blossom. There are not even enough words to say thank you for walking with me on this journey — I'm grateful for the many miles and many years we've shared as colleagues and friends. Your talents and generosity are boundless!

Thank you to my first readers: Andrea, Kirsten, Kris, and Marisa. Your generous sharing of insights, love, and encouragement has been invaluable.

Andrea, Chisom, Jennie, Clara, Dea, and Lizzie: Thank you for being in the journey as the vision came into sight.

And to my sweetest dad who I miss deeply, I endlessly thank you. People always said I was your carbon copy, for which I have become more deeply grateful every day. Thank you for your guidance, tenderness, love, words of wisdom, and especially for letting me also find my own way.

A handwritten note from my dad that he wrote to me when I was traversing some rough waters… shared with you here with the love and gentleness that my dad embodied.

Keep a cool head & A warm heart

Converse with Care

Take good care of yourself and each other as you engage with this book. This care guide is provided not to prescribe what you discuss, but how. Time together is precious; even in a few moments, you can ignite what is radically possible. These are conversations to tend to with care.

Here are a few suggestions:

1. Arrive having nourished yourself. Be present on your terms and aware of how you are feeling both physically, emotionally, and mentally as you enter into conversation.

2. Start by taking a few deep breaths together before you begin the conversation.

3. Gather your thoughts, perhaps through journaling or jotting down notes.

4. Welcome each other by asking an opening question such as:

    a. What are you bringing with you today?

    b. What is top of mind or top of heart for you?

    c. What is distracting you, and what is bringing you relief today?

5. Open up the conversation with your initial thoughts and reflections about this book.

6. You are in this exploration together, but also remember that you are each on your own journeys. Acknowledge the

offerings fellow participants are making, including your own. Build and generate the conversation together.

7. Remember that you self-determine how you show up. You don't have to tell your story or share anything you don't want to, and you can still participate.

8. Be curious about different perspectives and experiences. Create spaciousness to explore without having to agree.

9. Close your time together in this conversation with a comment about learning and gratitude.

Reviews

Bina's generous and practical offering is one so deeply needed as I seek to replenish my energy to stay the course on the arc towards justice. Say The Quiet Part Out Loud is part manifesto, part journal, and an aunty-sized kick in pants. Most importantly, it is an invitation to find grace, move towards joy and purposeful action within myself and alongside others.

Kris Archie CEO
The Circle on Philanthrophy

Bina says the quiet part out loud with courage and love. She is giving us tools and beckoning us to walk with purpose….to reckon with the rage we often feel while working towards advancing justice and to move forward with a more open heart. That my rage is actually my love is highly provocative. This little big book is a guide that I will reach for, for a long time.

Marisa Aurora Quiroz, President & CEO
International Community Foundation

It is rare to read practical guides that both hold us close to our sense of individualism as well as collectivism. Say the Quiet Part Out Loud is a resounding call to identify and continuously release the ways in which white supremacy silences, and separates us.

Kirsten Scobie, Founder and Principal
Persimmon Consulting Co.